NEW ENGLAND
ICONS AND INSPIRATIONS
BY TOMMY HILFIGER

RIZZOLI
NEW YORK

NEW ENGLAND

I f I had to name my greatest source of inspiration, it would be New England. To me, it is the heart and soul of America. It's where our country was born. Our style, our traditions, our icons—the things that are distinctly American in spirit and design—originated in the Northeast. New England is the birthplace of our heritage, from Plymouth Rock to the site of the Boston Tea Party. It is home to some of our most sophisticated cities, quaintest towns, and oldest seafaring communities. New England is the real deal. If you want to see, touch, taste, and experience quintessential America, you only need visit New England.

New England has it all: rocky coastlines and sandy beaches. Picturesque lighthouses, stunning green mountains. Competitive skiing, world-class sailing. White picket fences, low stone walls. Stately Georgian houses, simple clapboard cottages. The best lobster and chowder on the planet, unbeatable blueberry pies. Labrador retrievers and woody station wagons. Rugged fishermen and tweedy scholars. New England is the land of polo fields and dairy farms; of the elegantly plain and the gracefully complex.

I love New England in all its extremes, including the weather. The summers are gloriously sunny, the winters snowy and white. Each season brings its own trove of treasures. There's no choosing between a weekend of sailing off the coast of Maine and a weekend of skiing in Vermont. Nor must you decide between a clambake on Martha's Vineyard and home-cooked duck in front of a fireplace at a New Hampshire inn. Opportunities present themselves according to season, such

as walking through Provincetown when the leaves start turning and antiquing in Newport come the spring. You need to experience it all. If you can throw in a Red Sox game or watch Yale and Harvard compete, all the better.

There's an integrity to New England's style which comes from its authenticity. Think of the clothing: tweed jackets with leather elbow patches. Pea coats and Shetland sweaters. Button-down Oxford shirts and striped ties. Chinos and boat shoes. Fisherman cable knits and penny loafers. These stalwarts of style were founded on quality and function and only later became fashion. Clothes don't get older in New England, they get better and then handed down. Laundered, worn, frayed-around-the-edges—these traits only enhance the look. In New England, younger generations don't run from tradition, they embrace it. Good taste prevails. Just look at the architecture: a Cape Cod shingle, a New England colonial, even the modest log cabin or simple red barn. The graphic lines of quilts and nautical flags. Then there is the all-American palette that's always in style: Nantucket Red, Puritan White, and True Blue. New England style, in all its forms, endures.

Most enduring is New England's sense of family. It can be a traditional place when it comes to values and ethics. Families work hard and have dinner together. Neighbors are always quick to lend a hand. New Englanders are a hardy lot, many with large, extended families—something I relate to being the oldest boy of nine children, and now the father of four. Maybe it's the fierce winters that keep everyone gathered indoors or the beautiful summers that call us to saltboxes on the shore. Or perhaps it's the russet-toned autumns that invite touch football on the lawn. Pastimes are family-oriented: apple-picking, hay rides, canoeing, camping—good, wholesome fun. There's something safe and homey about New England.

New England cultivates character. It is as youthful as it is venerable, as modern as it is historic. Its renowned Ivy League universities nurture the thinkers of tomorrow. Creatively, New England is fertile ground. Some of our country's greatest innovators, past and present, have called it home: John Quincy Adams and John F. Kennedy, style setters Sister Parish, Babe Paley, and C. Z. Guest, iconic American artists like Winslow Homer and Katharine Hepburn, writers as diverse as Walt Whitman, Robert Frost, and Stephen King, and musicians like Arlo Guthrie, James Taylor, and Aerosmith.

Norman Rockwell spent most of his life in Vermont and Massachusetts. A hero of mine, Rockwell celebrated everyday American life. He cherished little moments, be it a girl showing off a missing tooth, a boy's first haircut, or a young couple sharing a soda pop after the prom. He grasped the simple pleasure of gathering around the Thanksgiving table. He saw the quiet joy in fishing and the innocent exuberance of baseball. Is it any wonder his nostalgic images have come to represent our country at its most ideal?

Admittedly, I have a romantic vision of New England. It has been home to many of the good times in my life. I am raising my family in Connecticut and have a summer house on Nantucket. I love to ski in Vermont. I started my career on Cape Cod at a small boutique called The Sunflower, and my company's first photo shoot was at Moosehead Lake. New England's clean, preppy, athletic style has always been the cornerstone of my designs. It's a look that unites the young and old, the aristocrat and the working man. It's a style that invites everyone to the party, to come join the team. The New England spirit is inclusive. It's a true classic; it was here before us and will live on long after we're gone. That is why I love New England—my joy, my muse, my home.

— Tommy Hilfiger

I see New England as a snapshot of the American landscape. It has it all:

seaside tranquility, mountain ruggedness, and big-city sophistication.

LANDSCAPE

The one great poem
of New England is her Sunday.

LITCHFIELD COUNTY

CONNECTICUT

My soul is full of longing
For the secret of the Sea,
And the heart of the great ocean
Sends a thrilling pulse through me.

HENRY WADSWORTH LONGFELLOW (1807–1882)
FROM "THE SECRET OF THE SEA" (1850)

PENOBSCOT BAY

MAINE

BLOCK ISLAND

RHODE ISLAND

Summer is the time
when one sheds one's tensions
with one's clothes, and the right kind of day
is jeweled balm for the battered spirit.
A few of those days and you can become drunk
with the belief that all's right with the world.

ADA LOUISE HUXTABLE (B. 1921)
ON VACATIONING IN NEW ENGLAND.

BOSTON

MASSACHUSETTS

I want to tell you about the town of Stockbridge, Massachusetts... they got three stop signs, two police officers, and one police car.

ARLO GUTHRIE (B. 1947)
FROM "ALICE'S RESTAURANT" (1967)

To me, New England is about wholesome fun. Whether it's sailing, skiing, or the peacefulness of a long walk,

New England's pastimes embrace the beauty of nature and feed the soul.

LEISURE

Go confidently
in the direction of your dreams!
Live the life you've imagined.
As you simplify your life,
the laws of the universe
will be simpler.

All literary men
are Red Sox fans — to be a Yankee fan
in a literate society is to endanger your life.

JOHN CHEEVER (1912–1982)

STOWE

VERMONT

The most serious charge which can be brought against New England is not Puritanism but February.

JOSEPH WOOD KRUTCH (1893–1970)
FROM "TWELVE SEASONS" (1949)

MARTHA'S VINEYARD

MASSACHUSETTS

Paris' rooftops were lovely to see
Switzerland's vertical landscape
Crossed my mind's eye just now
Canada's shoreline has been calling out to me
But it's been too long a time
Since last I crossed
That vast Nantucket sound

JAMES TAYLOR (B. 1948)
FROM "HELLO OLD FRIEND" (1974)

NANTUCKET

MASSACHUSETTS

Prior to the nineteenth century,
only widows, orphans, and servants ate lobster.
And in some parts of New England, serving lobster
to prison inmates more than once a week
was forbidden by law, as doing so
was considered cruel and unusual punishment.

LINDA GREENLAW (B. 1960)
FROM *THE LOBSTER CHRONICLES* (2002)

The New England conscience ... does not stop you from doing what you shouldn't it just stops you from enjoying it.

CLEVELAND AMORY (1917–1998)

New England's architecture is designed to weather storms and stand for hundreds of years.

There's a forever-ness about the clean, classic lines and hardy materials.

SHELTER

SOUTH BERWICK

MAINE

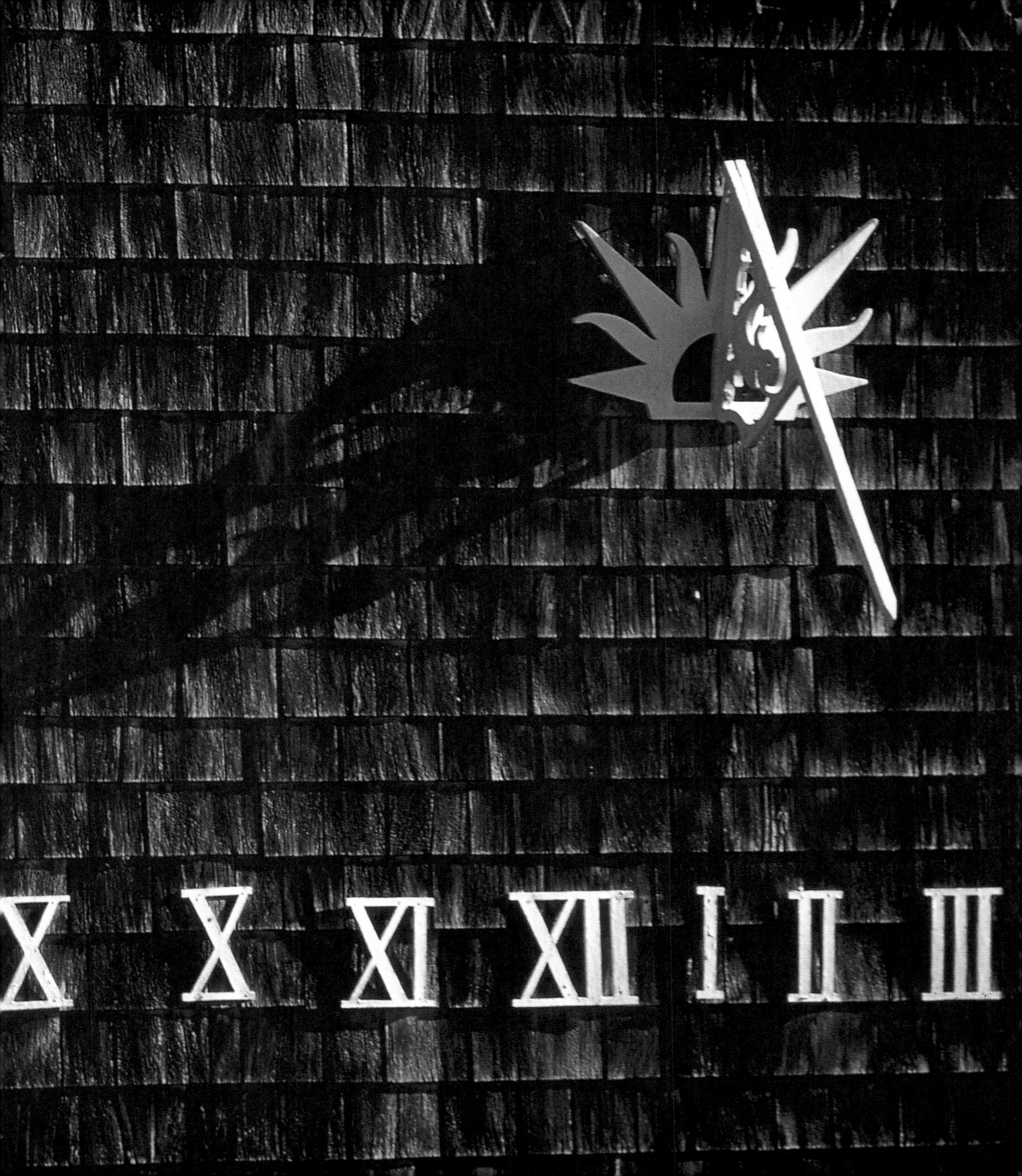
X X XI XII I II III

Proportion
is the good breeding of architecture.

EDITH WHARTON (1862–1937) AND OGDEN CODMAN, JR. (1853–1951)
FROM *THE DECORATION OF HOUSES* (1902)

Commuter-
one who spends his life
In riding to and from his wife;
A man who shaves and takes a train,
And then rides back to shave again.

E. B. WHITE (1899–1985)

FROM *POEMS AND SKETCHES OF E. B. WHITE* (1925)

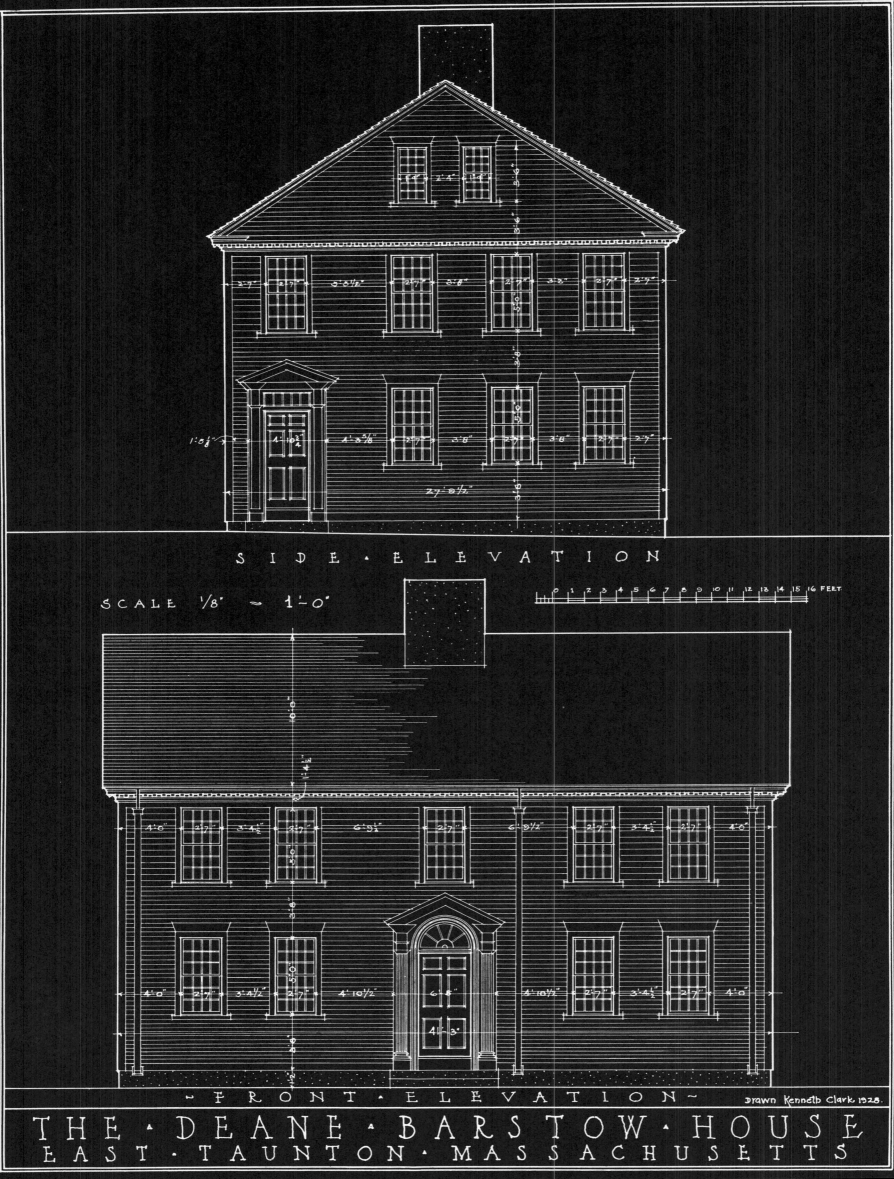

S I D E · E L E V A T I O N

SCALE ⅛" = 1'-0"

0 1 2 3 4 5 6 7 8 9 10 11 12 13 14 15 16 FEET

~ F R O N T · E L E V A T I O N ~

Drawn Kenneth Clark 1928

T H E · D E A N E · B A R S T O W · H O U S E
E A S T · T A U N T O N · M A S S A C H U S E T T S

SHELBURNE

VERMONT

And o'er them
the lighthouse looked lovely as hope—
That star of life's tremulous ocean.

PAUL MOON JAMES (1780–1854)
FROM "THE BEACON"

 **BATES**

BENNINGTON COLLEGE

NN.

COLBY

 **MOUNT HOLYOKE COLLEGE**

 **UNIVERSITY OF NEW HAMPSHIRE**

MASSACHUSETTS INSTITUTE OF TECHNOLOGY

 **YALE UNIVERSITY**

 **TUFTS**

 **UNIVERSITY OF VERMONT**

AMHERST

BROWN

BOWDOIN

BRANDEIS
UNIVERSITY

field

SON

HARVARD

PINE MANOR
COLLEGE

TRINITY
COLLEGE

Bantams

WILLIAMS

CONNECTICUT
COLLEGE

BOSTON UNIVERSITY

BOSTON COLLEGE

Fair

DARTMOUTH

EMERS

UNIVERSITY OF **RI** RHODE ISLAND.

COAST GUARD ACADEMY

WELLESLEY COLLEGE

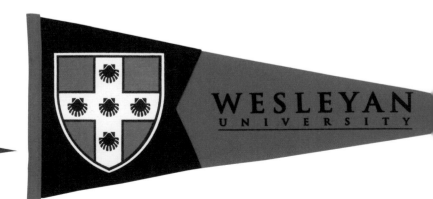

WESLEYAN UNIVERSITY

The wide oak planks of the floor, rounded and buckled here and there, and the magnificent hand-hewn beams, were obviously unchanged since Revolutionary times. But the furnishings were in general of the era of Benjamin Harrison, with an overlay of William McKinley, and here and there a final, crowning touch of Calvin Coolidge.

ERIC HODGINS (1899–1971)
FROM *MR. BLANDINGS BUILDS HIS DREAM HOUSE* (1946)

Halfway down a by-street of one of our New England towns stands a rusty wooden house, with seven acutely peaked gables, facing towards various points of the compass, and a huge, clustered chimney in the midst.

NATHANIEL HAWTHORNE (1804–1864)
FROM *THE HOUSE OF SEVEN GABLES* (1851)

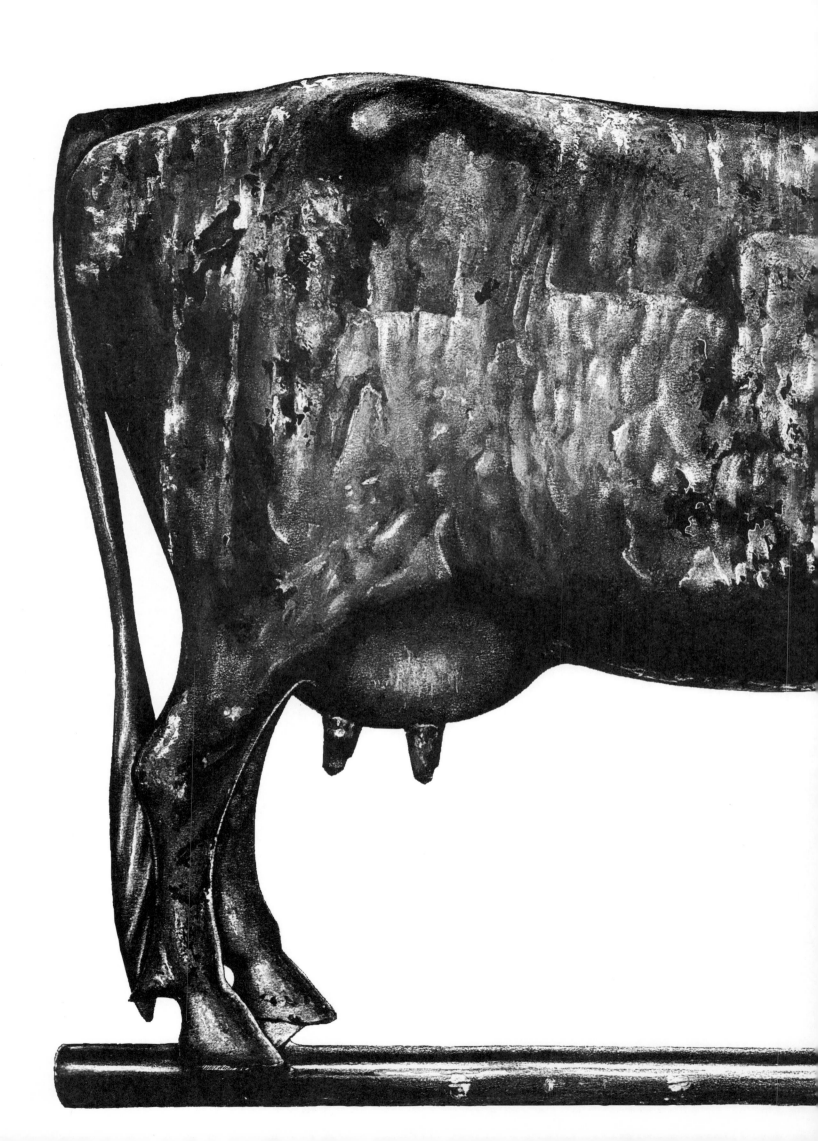

The main purpose of a door is to admit, its secondary purpose is to exclude.

EDITH WHARTON (1862–1937) AND OGDEN CODMAN, JR. (1853–1951)
FROM *THE DECORATION OF HOUSES* (1902)

In New England, style is never about what's "in" or "out."

STYLE

New England
is the home of all that is good
and noble with all her sternness
and uncompromising opinions.

ELLEN HENRIETTA SWALLOW RICHARDS (1842–1911)

LINCOLNVILLE

MAINE

CANTERBURY

NEW HAMPSHIRE

There are two types of education... One should teach us how to make a living, and the other how to live.

Searching my heart for its true sorrow,
This is the thing I find to be:
That I am weary of words and people,
Sick of the city, wanting the sea;

Wanting the sticky, salty sweetness
Of the strong wind and shattered spray;
Wanting the loud sound and the soft sound
Of the big surf that breaks all day.

EDNA ST. VINCENT MILLAY (1892–1950)
FROM "EXILED" (1921)

Without
discipline, there's no life at all.

WESTPORT

CONNECTICUT

At the end of an hour we saw
a far-away town sleeping in a valley
by a winding river; and beyond it on a hill,
a vast gray fortress, with towers and turrets,
the first I had ever seen out of a picture.

"Bridgeport?" said I, pointing.

"Camelot," said he.

MARK TWAIN (1835–1910)
FROM *A CONNECTICUT YANKEE IN KING ARTHUR'S COURT* (1889)

COLUMBIA FALLS

MAINE

New England connects us all through its traditions, from great colleges

and sporting history, to time-honored trades and professions.

TRADITION

Listen my children and you shall hear
Of the midnight ride of Paul Revere,
On the eighteenth of April, in Seventy-five;
Hardly a man is now alive
Who remembers that famous day and year.

HENRY WADSWORTH LONGFELLOW (1807–1882)
FROM "THE MIDNIGHT RIDE OF PAUL REVERE" (1860)

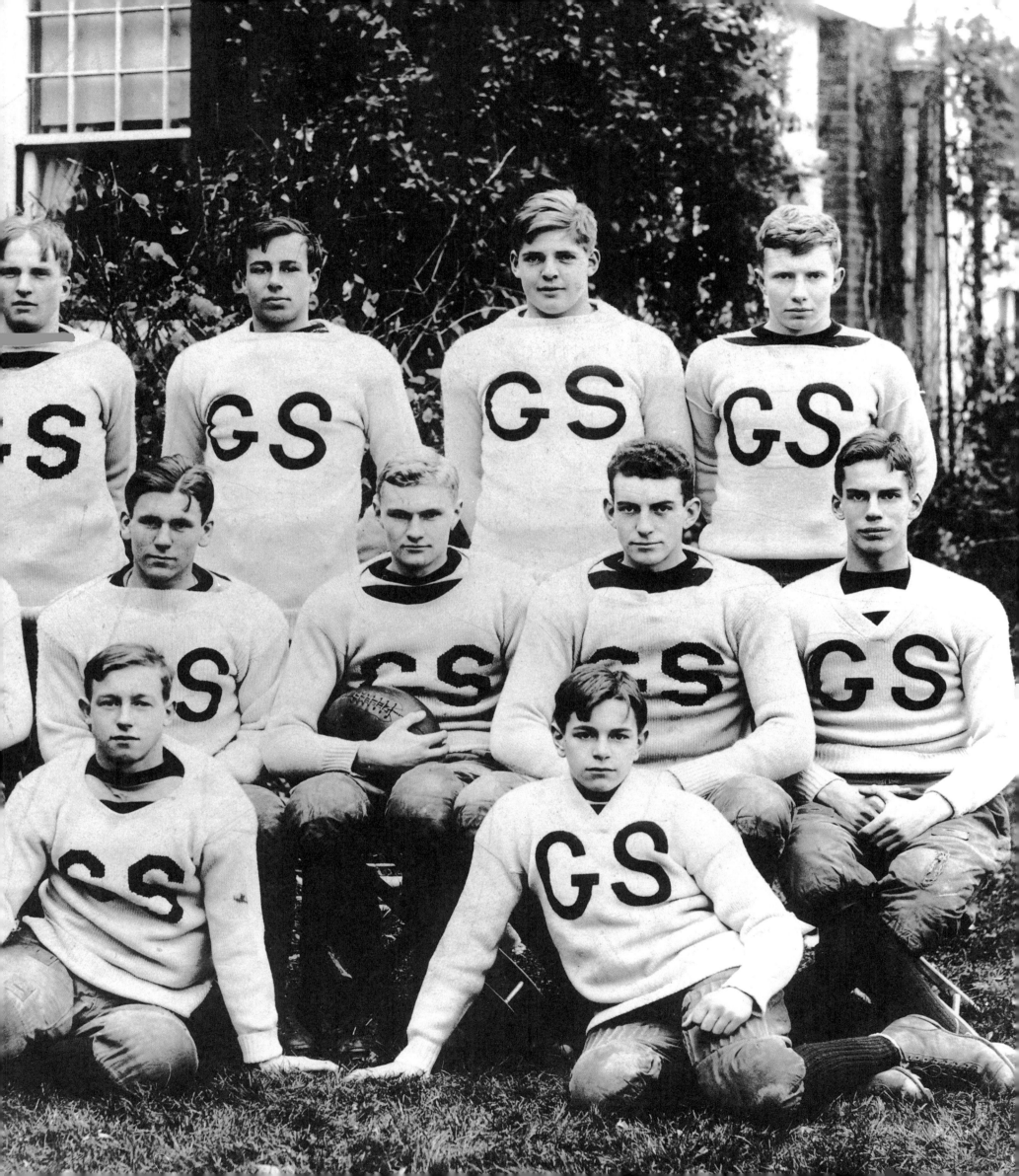

A whale-ship was my Yale College and my Harvard.

HERMAN MELVILLE (1819–1891)
FROM *MOBY DICK* (1851)

Menu for
New England Thanksgiving Dinner

Oyster Soup
Crisp Crackers

Celery
Salted Almonds

Roast Stuffed Turkey
Giblet Gravy
Cranberry Jelly

Mashed Potatoes
Onions in Cream
Turnips

Chicken Pie

Thanksgiving Pudding
Sterling Sauce

Mince, Apple, and
Squash Pie

Fruit
Nuts and Raisins
Bonbons

Vanilla Ice Cream
Fancy Cakes

Cheese and Crackers
Café Noir

FANNIE MERRITT FARMER (1857–1915)
FROM *THE BOSTON COOKING-SCHOOL COOK BOOK* (1918)

i thank You God for most this amazing day: for the leaping greenly spirits of trees and a blue true dream of sky; and for everything which is natural which is infinite which is yes

E. E. CUMMINGS (1894-1962)
FROM "I THANK YOU GOD FOR MOST THIS AMAZING" (1950)

If we mean to have heroes, statesmen, and philosophers, we should have learned women.

ABIGAIL ADAMS (1744–1818)

When a resolute young fellow
steps up to the great bully, the world,
and takes him boldly by the beard,
he is often surprised to find it comes off in his hand,
and that it was only tied on to scare
away the timid adventurers.

RALPH WALDO EMERSON (1803–1882)

NEWPORT

RHODE ISLAND

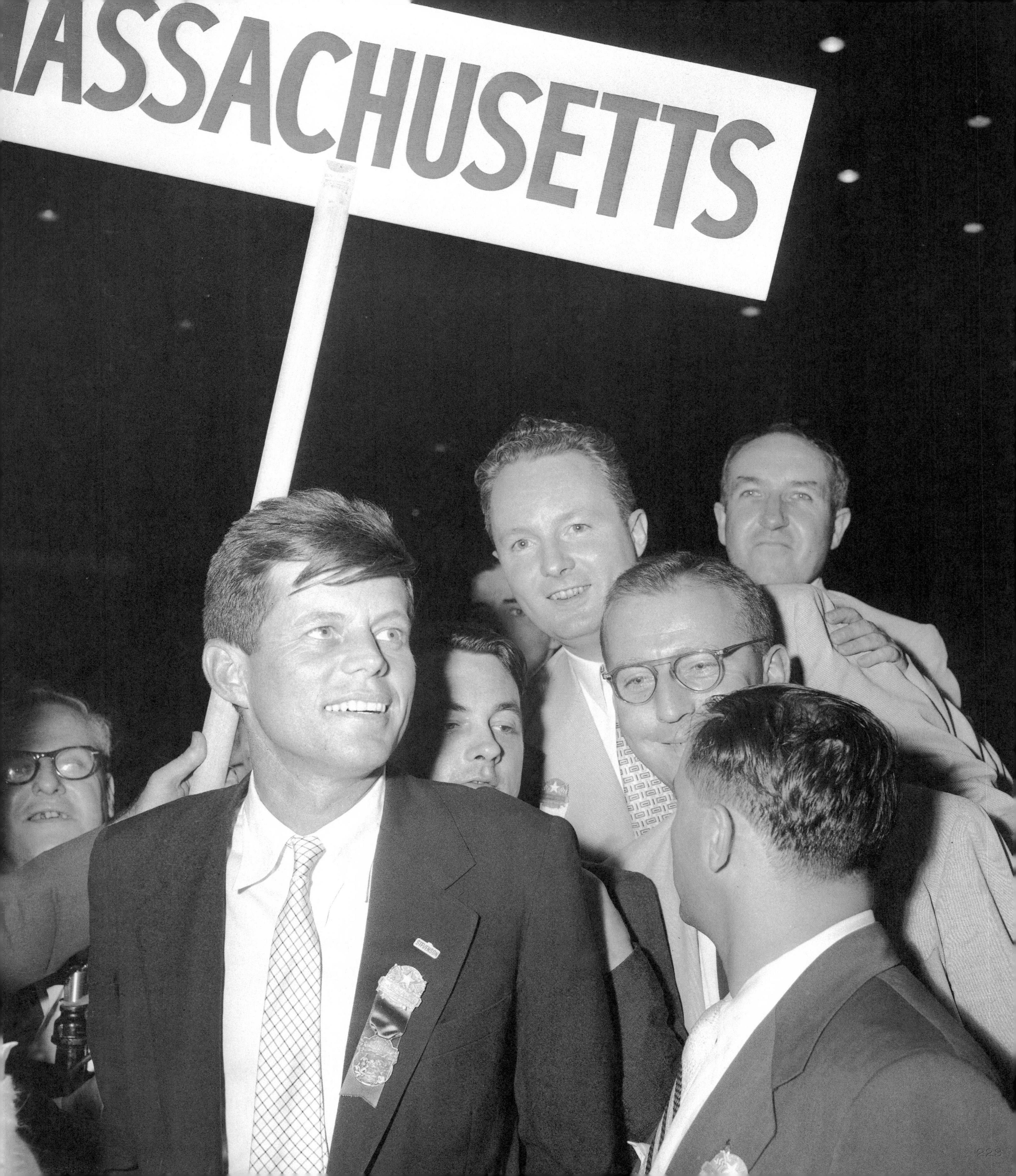
ASSACHUSETTS
STEVENSON

Conventional wisdom
not withstanding, there is no reason
either in football or in poetry why the two
should not meet in a man's life
if he has the weight and cares
about the words.

ARCHIBALD MACLEISH (1892–1982)

strated W
1728 by

Volume 201, Number 21

Nov. 24, '28

5 cts.

10c. in Canada

225

The house of my birth was quaint, with clapboards running up and down, neatly trimmed; there were five rooms, a tiny porch, a rosy front yard, and unbelievably delicious strawberries in the rear.

W. E. B. DUBOIS (1868–1963)

FROM *THE AUTOBIOGRAPHY OF W. E. B. DUBOIS: A SOLILOQUY ON VIEWING MY LIFE FROM THE LAST DECADE OF ITS FIRST CENTURY* (1968)

The land is holy where they fought
And holy where they fell;
For by their blood that land was bought,
The land they loved so well.

ISAAC MCLELLAN (1806–1899)
FROM "NEW ENGLAND'S DEAD" (1900)

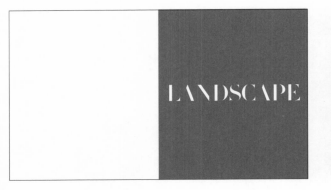

LANDSCAPE

View from "Fortune Rock," ca. 1939. House designed by American architect George Howe on Mount Desert Island, Maine. (Photo by Ben Schnall)

Lighthouse Hill by Edward Hopper, 1927. A native New Yorker, Hopper summered at the New England coast where he became enamored with lighthouses. This painting was made while on vacation with his wife, Jo, in Maine. The Cape Elizabeth lighthouse and keeper's cottage look much the same today, though the surrounding landscape has since been developed.

T he one great poem of New England is her Sunday.

Mrs. James Watson Webb with her daughter, Mrs. Dunbar Bostwick, and four grandchildren at their family farm along Lake Champlain, Vermont, 1944. Electra Havemeyer Webb started the Shelburne Museum in Vermont in 1947. The museum features art, Americana, artifacts, and architecture on forty-five acres. (Photo by Toni Frissell)

Trotting Cracks on Snow, Currier & Ives, 1858. Calling themselves "Printmakers to the People," the print house founded by Massachusetts-born Nathaniel Currier and James Ives used staff artists as well as established ones. From 1835 to 1907, they produced in excess of 7,500 different titles, totaling over one million prints.

The Webb Deane Stevens Museum in Weathersfield, Connecticut. A group of historical homes, including the red Webb House, built in 1752 by merchant Joseph Webb, are early examples of clapboard architecture, a quintessentially New England building style. It was at the Webb House where George Washington planned the final battle of the Revolutionary War. (Photo by Michael Freeman)

Fall foliage in the historic village of Peacham, Vermont, settled in 1776. (Photo by William H. Johnson)

LITCHFIELD COUNTY

American playwright Arthur Miller and his wife, photographer Inge Morath at their home in Roxbury, Connecticut, 1962. (Photo by Dennis Stock)

Field of lupine in Sugar Hill, New Hampshire, with view of the White Mountain Presidential Range. The range includes Mount Washington (elevation 6,288 feet), the highest peak in the northeastern United States. (Photo by Paul Rezendes)

Nineteenth-century weathervane. The rooster is probably the earliest weathervane design in this country. The motif was widely used in Europe, where the cock was featured on church steeples to reference Peter's denial of Christ, and thus served as a warning to the congregation not to do likewise.

Three young "farm hands," brothers James Verrill, Jr., Scott, and Christopher of Bangor, Maine, appear to be pushing giant rolls of hay in this Troy field late in August ca. 1978. The hay was rolled up by farm machinery earlier in the week.

*M*y soul is full of longing
For the secret of the sea,
And the heart of the great ocean
Sends a thrilling pulse through me.

PENOBSCOT BAY

Mrs. Hans Estin and Mrs. Leverett Saltonstall Shaw with Mrs. Shaw's children on Black Beach, a favorite clamming spot at low tide. Manchester, Massachusetts, late 1950s. (Photo by Slim Aarons)

Overcast skies and a board fence frame the small town of Stonington, Connecticut, 1940. A charming seaport, Stonington is located on the southeastern corner of Connecticut and has over 350 years of recorded history. Stonington was home to Nathaniel B. Palmer, the seafarer credited with discovering Antarctica. (Photo by Jack Delano)

Maine islands, 1993. Off the coast of Maine are more than 3000 islands, both publicly and privately owned. (Photo by Jed Wilcox)

BLOCK ISLAND

Bostwick Farm, Shelburne, Vermont. Dunbar W. Bostwick with his prize trotting horse and Dalmatian, ca. 1960. Both the horse and dog answer to the same name, Chris Spencer. (Photo by Slim Aarons)

Eliot Porter (1901–1990) introduced color to landscape photography. An artist with strong scientific and environmental interests, Porter took up color in 1939, long before his fellow photographers accepted it, to produce more accurate photographs of birds. Soon thereafter, he expanded his focus to celebrate the colorful beauty of nature in general. Porter found great inspiration and subjects for his photography on Great Spruce Head Island, Maine, where his family had a summerhouse. (Photo by Eliot Porter)

North American Indians, including the woodland tribes of New England, are responsible for creating the classic version of the canoe—a frame of wooden ribs covered with the lightweight bark of birch, and sometimes elm or cedar trees. These boats, which have remained virtually unchanged in design for thousands of years, have in recent times adopted more resilient materials such as metal and fiberglass. (Photo by Josef Scaylea)

Block Island North Light, Rhode Island. Block Island, sometimes called the "Bermuda of the North," has also long been known for its dangerous shoals and frequent fog. Between 1819 and 1838, fifty-nine vessels were wrecked on or near the island. (Photo by Paul Rezendes)

*S*ummer is the time when one sheds one's tensions with one's clothes, and the right kind of day is jeweled balm for the battered spirit. A few of those days and you can become drunk with the belief that all's right with the world.

Wild blueberry picking. Maine's official state berry was first commercially harvested in the 1840s. The state now produces twenty-five percent of all blueberries in North America. Grown across 60,000 acres, Maine's blueberry industry produces an annual crop of some sixty-five million pounds, valued at more than seventy-five million dollars. (Photo by Amy Toensing)

Nantucket, playing in field of Queen Anne's lace, 1970. Children are descendants of early Cape Verdean settlers. The whaling trade brought sailors to Nantucket from all over the world, from Africa as well as Portugal and Great Britain. The windmill in the background was built in 1764 from timbers of shipwrecks. (Photo by James L. Stanfield)

Miss Mildred McCormick's early nineteenth-century village house, Bar Harbor, Maine, 1909. The garden was designed by Beatrix Farrand, the famed garden designer and founding member of the American Society of Landscape Architects. McCormick's charming garden features border dahlias, delphiniums, baby's breath, lilies, and many colorful annuals.

BOSTON

Old North Church, Boston. Built in 1723, The Old North Church is classic Georgian style. Two lanterns associated with Paul Revere were hung from the church's steeple by Robert Newman, church sexton, on April 18, 1775, igniting the War for Independence. The Old North Church is part of the Episcopal Diocese of Massachusetts.

Birch trees surround the former home of President Calvin Coolidge in Plymouth, Vermont. In addition to being Coolidge's birthplace, childhood residence, and final resting site, Plymouth Notch was also where the vacationing Vice President received word of President Harding's death. On August 3, 1923, Coolidge was sworn in as the thirtieth president of the United States at the family homestead by his notary public father.
(Photo by Raymond Gehman)

Tully River during a December snowstorm. Royalston, Massachusetts, 2002.
(Photo by Paul Rezendes)

I want to tell you about the town of Stockbridge Massachusets... they got three stop signs, two police officers, and one police car.

Norman Rockwell walking with his dogs in Vermont, 1950. America's foremost illustrator of small-town life, Rockwell lived in Arlington, Vermont and later Stockbridge, Massachusetts (both states have Rockwell museums). Rockwell's forty-seven-year career produced more than 4,000 illustrations, 332 of which were covers of *The Saturday Evening Post*.

Sheffield Island Lighthouse, Connecticut, 1972. Retaining walls provide barriers to down slope movement of soil, rock, or water— all common concerns throughout the craggy landscape of New England. They are generally made of masonry, though in recent years railroad ties, shown here, have been a popular material.
(Photo by James L. Amos)

LEISURE

The topsail schooner Shenandoah approaching Brant Point in the Nantucket Sound, 1970. This lighthouse has guided seafarers since 1764.
(Photo by James L. Stanfield)

Go confidently in the direction of your dreams! Live the life you've imagined. As you simplify your life, the laws of the universe will be simpler.

Husband and wife radio personalities Edward (1898–1982) and Pegeen Fitzgeral (1910–1989) found respite from their hectic New York lives in the woods of rural Connecticut. A devoted animal lover, Pegeen founded the Last Post Animal Sanctuary in 1982 on thirty-seven acres in Falls Village on the Housatonic River in the foot-hills of the Berkshires.
(Photo by Slim Aarons)

Swift Diamond River, Great North Woods, New Hampshire.
(Photo by Paul Rezendes)

Fisherman casting in Dead River, Maine, 1930.
(Photo by Philip Gendreau)

All literary men are Red Sox fans to be a Yankee fan in a literate society is to endanger your life.

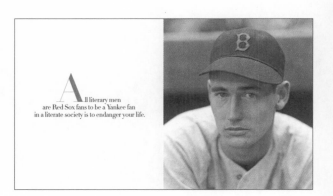

Ted Williams, outfielder for the Boston Red Sox, 1941. Williams played with the Red Sox for nineteen seasons, retiring at age forty-two. During his major league career, Williams was named American League Most Valuable Player twice, achieved two AL Triple Crowns, won six AL batting championships, and is considered one of the greatest hitters with 521 homeruns and a lifetime average of .344. He was inducted into the Hall of Fame in 1966.

Sails of the USA racing yacht, 1986. (Photo by Roger Ressmeyer)

Harold S. Vanderbilt at the wheel of his yacht, Ranger, as he prepares to defend the America's Cup on June 18, 1937 off of Newport, Rhode Island.

Still from the film *Way Down East*, 1935, starring Henry Fonda and Rochelle Hudson, shown here leading an ice-skating line.

Young skier in Stowe, Vermont. Stowe (chartered in 1763) is the largest town in land area in Vermont with over 50,000 acres. The state's highest peak, Mt. Mansfield, is located here and has been a playground for generations of skiers. The sport was first introduced here by three resident Swedish families in 1913.(Photo by Slim Aarons)

STOWE

Film still from *Parrish*, 1961. Directed by Delmar Dave, starring Colette Colbert and Tab Hunter, shown here with actress Alison Post. The story is centered on a tobacco plantation in the Connecticut River valley.

Lifeguard stand, Ballston Beach, Cape Cod, Massachusetts, 1976. The Cape Cod National Seashore comprises 43,604 acres of shoreline, including a forty-mile long stretch of pristine sandy beach. Among New England's most beloved destinations, "the Cape" (as it's affectionately called) offers six swimming beaches, eleven self-guiding nature trails, and a variety of picnic areas and scenic overlooks. (Photo by Joel Meyerowitz)

T he most serious charge that can be brought against New England is not Puritanism but February.

Students from Stowe Preparatory School track through deep snow near Mount Mansfield and Spruce Peak, Vermont, ca. 1960. (Photo by Slim Aarons)

A teenage sailor helps maneuver an Indian sailboat in a race at the Nantucket Yacht Club, 1970. (Photo by James L. Stanfield)

MARTHA'S VINEYARD

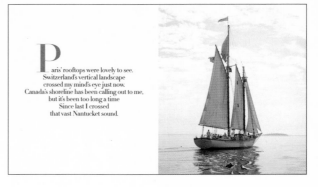

Boy running, Martha's Vineyard, Massachusetts. Seven miles off the coast of Massachusetts, Martha's Vineyard is 100 square miles and composed of six towns. In 1602, English explorer Bartholomew Gosnaldo named it after his mother-in-law who helped finance his voyage and the island's signature wild grapevines. (Photo by William Abranowicz)

White Birches in the Snow, 1931. Painting by Maxfield Parrish (1870–1966). Following a visit to his parents' home in Cornish, New Hampshire in 1894, Parrish and his wife, Lydia, purchased land in nearby Plainfield, becoming full-time residents in 1898. Parrish designed and built his home, The Oaks, and soon became an active member of the Cornish Colony of artists.

Model on snowshoes, 1924. American Indians are credited for innovating the snowshoe, in fact, nearly every American Indian tribe has its own particular shape of shoe. (Photo by Edward Steichen)

P aris' rooftops were lovely to see. Switzerland's vertical landscape crossed my mind's eye just now. Canada's shoreline has been calling out to me, but it's been too long a time Since last I crossed that vast Nantucket sound.

The Appledore schooner leaving Camden harbor in West Penobscot Bay, Maine. (Photo by Paul Rezendes)

Members of the Historic American Buildings Survey assembled for a campfire near Great Point Light, Nantucket, 1970. (Photo by James L. Stanfield)

Milt Schmidt, captain of the Boston Bruins, 1953. Milton Conrad Schmidt is best known as the center for the Bruins in the 1930s and 40s. Milt was a prime force in the Bruins' Stanley Cup Championships of 1939 and 1941. In 1940, Milt won the Art Ross Trophy as the NHL's leading scorer.

Students at Plymouth State Teachers College, New Hampshire, square dancing in their "raquettes" or snowshoes, 1955. (Photo by Orlando)

NANTUCKET

Thirty miles off Cape Cod, Nantucket is an idyllic "elbow of sand," where inland, the wild moors open to the endless sky. Named a National Historic District, nearly forty percent of the island is protected conservation land. (Photo by Joel Grey)

Sugaring on Frank H. Shurtleff's farm that was purchased by his grandfather one-hundred years earlier, North Bridgewater, Vermont, 1940. Vermont is the largest producer of maple syrup and sugar in the United States, producing some forty percent of the total U.S. crop. The climate is ideal for growing maple trees as it is for enabling a good sap flow. Cultivation is key: forty years are required to grow a maple tree large enough to tap.

Summer tailgate picnic at the polo grounds, 1964. Polo was first played in the United States in 1876, introduced by newspaper publisher James Gordon Bennett, who had first seen the game played in England. Myopia Hunt Club in Hamilton, Massachusetts, the oldest continually-running polo club in the United States, hosted their first match in 1888. (Photo by Müller)

Prior to the nineteenth century, only widows, orphans, and servants ate lobster. And in some parts of New England, serving lobster to prison inmates more than once a week was forbidden by law, as doing so was considered cruel and unusual punishment.

Gourmet cover illustrated by Henry Stahlhut, 1945. Sometimes referred to as the king of seafood, Maine lobster is harvested from the icy, salt water of the North Atlantic and is distinctive for its mild and slightly sweet flavor.

The Harvard Varsity Crew team rows along the Charles River Basin as they get into shape for upcoming races in Boston, 1942. In the background are dormitories and other Harvard University buildings.

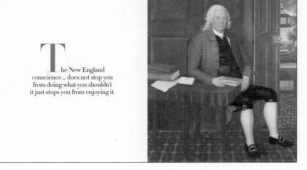

The New England conscience ... does not stop you from doing what you shouldn't it just stops you from enjoying it.

John Phillips founded Phillips Exeter Academy in 1783 in Exeter, New Hampshire. Portrait by Joseph Steward, 1793.

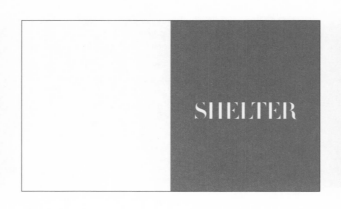

SHELTER

Bonnet from the front door of the Knight-Short House in Newburyport, Massachusetts. (Photo by Paul Rocheleau)

Hamilton House (ca. 1785), overlooking the Salmon Falls River, was lovingly restored to its former glory by Mrs. Emily Tyson and her stepdaughter, Elise, who purchased it in 1898. The historic house in South Berwick, Maine is now open to the public. (Photo by David Bohl)

The Young Men, Rhode Island, 1992. Known for her sharp-edged portraits of the East Coast leisure class, Barney lives and works out of Watch Hill, Rhode Island and New York City. (Photo by Tina Barney)

Built in 1907 at Robinson Point, Isle Au Haut Light was the last traditional-style lighthouse built in the state of Maine. Isle Au Haut or High Island was named by explorer Samuel de Champlain for its high elevation, the peak is 556 feet. The island only has about fifty year-round residents, with more in the summer. Most houses still don't have electricity. (Photo by Rick Lew)

Sundial on a shingled house in the fishing village of Siasconset, Nantucket, 1970. Nantucket is famous for its distinctive gray cedar shingle cottage, usually edged with white trim, wooden gutters, and a front porch. This popular style dates back to the Victorian era, when Nantucket first emerged as a summer community. (Photo by James L. Stanfield)

Proportion is the good breeding of architecture.

Architect Philip Johnson sitting outside of his renowned Glass House in New Caanan, Connecticut, 1999. Built in 1949, Johnson's steel and glass architectural home, thought to be one of the most beautiful but least functional houses, is considered a blueprint for modern architecture. (Photo by Richard Schulman)

Fine furniture production was a thriving business in early Boston and Newport. Two intermarried Quaker families—the Townsends and the Goddards—dominated eighteenth-century Newport cabinet-making, introducing such specifically North American design motifs as the lobed shell (many of which gracefully adorn this fine bonnet-top highboy).

Silas Dean House, Wethersfield, Connecticut. Ordered in 1766, this staircase with three different baluster patterns on each tread, is an excellent example of woodturning. The most striking corkscrewlike turning is characteristic of the English Cromwellian period. (Photo by Michael Freeman)

Hilltop Farm, Winter, 1949. Painting by Maxfield Parrish. Parrish drew inspiration from New Hampshire landscapes for many of his paintings, but he also cherished the privacy and lack of distractions of the small Connecticut River valley town of Plainfield.

Commuter—
one who spends his life
In riding to and from his wife;
A man who shaves and takes a train,
And then rides back to shave again.

Fashion model Wenda and two children pose as if greeting a commuter dad at a train station in Connecticut, ca. 1949. (Photo by Norman Parkinson)

Doorway of the ironmaster's house in the historic village of Saugus, Massachusetts. (Photo by Alex McLean)

Red Maple in Fall, Royalston, Massachusetts. (Photo by Paul Rezendes)

Side and front elevations of the Georgian-style Dean-Barstow House in East Taunton, Massachusetts, 1870.

Wallace Nutting chair. A former minister and avid photographer, devout New Englander Nuttingwas known for his line of fine antique reproductions, such as this Windsor Chair. Said Nutting, "Let nothing leave your hands till you are proud of it."

SHELBURNE

Mr. and Mrs. Samuel B. Webb in the trophy room at their home in Vermont, 1960. All the stuffed animals and birds in the room were shot by members of the family. Most notably, the large Alaskan brown bear on the right was shot by Mr. Webb's mother. (Photo by Slim Aarons)

The Old State House and State Street, Boston, by James Marston, ca. 1801. The imposing Old State house and the modern bow-fronted shops with residences above them attest to the easy commingling of public and private space in early Boston.

Glazed wool "Center Star" quilt, 1815–1825, New England. Quilting was not especially common in the average household until about 1840, when the textile industry had grown to the point that fabric was readily available to most families. Before that, colonial women spun their own cloth.

Covered sugar bowl in deep aqua glass inspired by Boston area glass houses, ca.1835–1855. The oldest town on Cape Cod, Sandwich was founded in 1637. Glassmaking brought notoriety and prosperity to this picturesque town in the nineteenth century. The Boston and Sandwich Glass Company (1825–1888) was located at Sandwich because of its abundance of local fuel (wood) and easy transportation. Their widely exported glass was influential in terms of style and technique in many parts of the growing country.

Mortgage button, Nantucket. Traditionally, when the mortgage was paid on a home, it was either rolled up or burned and placed inside a hole drilled in the top of the banister with a button over it. Mortgage buttons usually had the date scrimshawed on the back and the owner's initial on the top. (Photo by Alex McLean)

Emily Post's house and flower garden at Martha's Vineyard, Massachusetts, 1954. Roses and wisteria vines climb the walls with dahlias, phlox blooms, and the occasional campanulas. (Photo by Tom Leonard)

And o'er them the lighthouse looked lovely as hope - That star of life's tremulous ocean.

Mr. and Mrs. Charles B. P. Van Pelt, their son Peter and daughter Abby Ann by a lighthouse in Newport, Rhode Island, 1954. (Photo by Toni Frissell)

A large snow sculpture "replica" of the building it stands outside, at Dartmouth College, Hanover, New Hampshire, ca. 1955. Taken during the Dartmouth Winter Carnival that is still held every February. (Photo by John Titchen)

Yale quad, New Haven, Connecticut, 1964. Yale University was founded in 1701 as the Collegiate School in the home of Abraham Pierson, its first rector, in Killingworth, Connecticut. In 1716 the school moved to New Haven and, with the generous gift by Elihu Yale of nine bales of goods, 417 books, and a portrait of King George I, was renamed Yale College in 1718. (Photo by Joel Meyerowitz)

The wide oak planks of the floor, rounded and buckled here and there, and the magnificent hand-hewn beams, were obviously unchanged since Revolutionary times. But the furnishings were in general of the era of Benjamin Harrison, with an overlay of William McKinley, and here and there a final, crowning touch of Calvin Coolidge.

Still from *Mr. Blandings Builds His Dream House*, 1948. Starring Cary Grant and Myrna Loy.

Ferns are more than 300 million years old and have diversified into some 12,000 species worldwide. Over 100 fern varieties can be found in New England—from the whimsical (and edible) fiddlehead of the Ostrich Fern to the abundant Cinnamon Fern and delicate Polypody Fern which grows on rocks.

Pavilion on the grounds of Interior Designer Bunny Williams's home in northwest Connecticut. (Photo by Dana Gallagher)

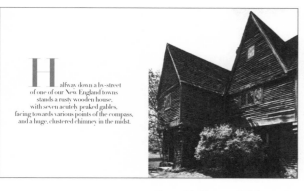

*H*alfway down a by-street of one of our New England towns stands a rusty wooden house, with seven acutely peaked gables, facing towards various points of the compass, and a huge, clustered chimney in the midst.

The gabled ironmaster's house in the historic village of Saugus, Massachusetts.
(Photo by Elliott Erwitt)

Members of the Cushing family opposite their house, The Ledges, in Newport, Rhode Island.
(Photo by Slim Aarons)

Cow weathervane, possibly made by Harris & Company, Boston, nineteenth-century. Though the use of weathervanes originated in Europe, the choice of animal motifs, particularly the cow, is characteristically American.

Still from the film *Summer Stock*, 1950. Directed by Charles Walters, starring Judy Garland and Gene Kelly. The story is centered on the Connecticut tradition of stock theater and the stage kitchen is a perfect replica of New England country style, Toby jugs and all.

*T*he main purpose of a door is to admit, its secondary purpose is to exclude.

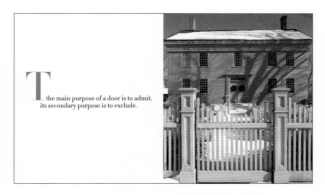

Berkshire County, Massachusetts, 1999. Built during the colonial era for a Boston settler, this house features an unadorned, classical facade with grand front door and a neat row of period sash windows.
(Photo by René Stoeltie)

STYLE

The Suits, 1977. Two New England summer favorites: seersucker suits and cocktail parties on the lawn.
(Photo by Tina Barney)

*N*ew England is the home of all that is good and noble with all her sternness and uncompromising opinions.

Mrs. Isaac Smith, 1769. Portrait by John Singleton Copley.

Compass card by Walter Folger, Jr. The fleur-de-lys was a common feature of the period, ca. 1790–1800.

Portrait of Joseph Winslow, 1806, by the Chinese painter, Spoilum. Whereas Chinese ancestor portraits traditionally confront the viewer full face, Spoilum's subjects present the oblique body angle and quizzicality of expression that seem to have an enduring appeal to the Western spectator. The effect is the more remarkable since, in all probability, Spoilum never traveled outside his native China and may never have met a professional artist from the West.

LINCOLNVILLE

CANTERBURY

Landscape artist Neil Welliver's house in Lincolnville, Maine. (Photo by Sølvi Dos Santos)

A classic white barn with black trim in North Haverhill, Grafton County, New Hampshire, 1964. (Photo by David Plowden)

Mrs. Stanley Grafton Mortimer, Jr. Later known simply as Babe Paley, the socialite Barbara Cushing Mortimer Paley was born in Boston, Massachusetts. She and her two sisters personified New England style. Paley went on to become a social icon, maintaining a position on the best-dressed list fourteen times before being inducted into the Fashion Hall of Fame in 1958.

Turned urn in front of a white house in Canterbury, New Hampshire. (Photo by Paul Rocheleau)

T here are two types of education... One should teach us how to make a living, and the other how to live.

S earching my heart for its true sorrow, This is the thing I find to be: That I am weary of words and people, Sick of the city, wanting the sea;

Wanting the sticky, salty sweetness Of the strong wind and shattered spray; Wanting the loud sound and the soft sound Of the big surf that breaks all day.

Charles Dana Gibson at his summer home near Dark Harbor, Maine, ca. 1940. Gibson was the illustrator behind the famed "Gibson Girl" look and style from the early twentieth century. (Photo by Luis Lemus)

Fore and Aft cottages, Truro, Cape Cod, Massachusetts, 1976. (Photo by Joel Meyerowitz)

Preppy trousers, Northeast Harbor, Maine, 2003. For leisure, New England men and boys have long embraced bold colors and prints. (Photo by Jennifer Livingston)

Jackie Kennedy, Hyannisport, Massachusetts, 1960. First Lady Jacqueline Lee Bouvier Kennedy was the epitome of New England chic. (Photo by Jacques Lowe)

W ithout discipline, there's no life at all.

Mr. and Mrs. Thomas Watson, Jr.—in patriotic red, white, and blue posing in front of their bi-plane in their garden in Maine, 1992. (Photo by Slim Aarons)

Born and raised in Hartford, Connecticut, Katharine Hepburn once said, "The single most important thing anyone needs to know about me is that I am totally, completely the product of two damn fascinating individuals who happened to be my parents." Her father was a prominent surgeon and her mother, a well-known political activist.

Model posing in front of a Boston-bound bus, 1938. (Photo by Toni Frissell)

Vogue skier. (Photo by Toni Frissell)

WESTPORT

Actors Paul Newman and Joanne Woodward at their home in Westport, Connecticut, 1965. At the Earthplace sanctuary in Westport, the Newman-Woodward Trail winds through an oak and beech forest. (Photo by Bruce Davidson)

Portrait of Elijah Boardman (1760–1823) by Ralph Earl (1751–1801). The dry-goods merchant is portrayed in his store in New Milford, Connecticut. Through the open paneled door to the right, bolts of textiles, including one with a prominently displayed British tax stamp, invite inspection and tell the viewer how Boardman earned a living, just as the books in his desk and the letter in his hand speak of his learning and awareness of culture.

As they sought to create their vision of "heaven on earth," the Shakers applied the virtues of simplicity, purity, and perfection to their work. Function and quality was emphasized in their products and designs, while their buildings were well constructed and appointed with efficient and modern amenities. The Shakers are credited with a number of innovations and inventions.

The "Golden Step" Room at Beauport in Gloucester, Massachusetts. The summer home of Henry Davis Sleeper, Beauport was described as "an intellectual fun house" because of its wit and delightful objects. The indoor terrace is dominated by a model of the square-rigger "Golden Step" for which the room is named. (Photo by David Bohl)

At the end of an hour we saw a far-away town sleeping in a valley by a winding river; and beyond it on a hill, a vast gray fortress, with towers and turrets, the first I had ever seen out of a picture.

"Bridgeport?" said I, pointing.

"Camelot," said he.

Mark Twain, Hartford, Connecticut, 1905. "Of all the beautiful towns it has been my fortune to see, (Hartford) is the chief . . . . You do not know what beauty is if you have not been there." Twain lived and worked in a nineteen-room, Tiffany-decorated, Hartford mansion from 1874 to 1891. During this period, Twain created such classics as *The Adventures of Tom Sawyer*, *The Adventures of Huckleberry Finn*, and *A Connecticut Yankee in King Arthur's Court*.

Nobska Light, Woods Hole, Massachusetts. Built in 1876, Nobska Light, located at the division between Buzzards Bay and Vineyard Sound is one of the most visible lighthouses of Cape Cod. (Photo by Paul Rezendes)

The daughter of a Massachusetts lawyer, Bette Davis was born in Lowell, Massachusetts. on April 5, 1908. The actress credited her solid Yankee heritage for making her tough enough to survive all that was required to be Hollywood star; she was also known for her clipped New England diction. (Photo by Erwin Blumenfeld)

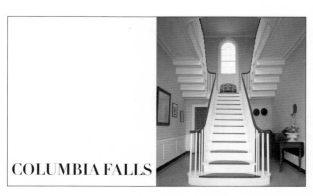

COLUMBIA FALLS

Stairhall at Ruggles House, Columbia Falls, Maine. (Photo by Paul Rocheleau)

Former U.S. president Calvin Coolidge drives a hay rake on his Plymouth, Vermont farm in 1931, two years after leaving the presidency.

TRADITION

Yale's oldest living graduate, New Haven, Connecticut, 1955. Founded in 1701, Yale has the distinction of having graduated five United States presidents. (Photo by Elliott Erwitt)

The Midnight Ride of Paul Revere, by Grant Wood, 1931. Wood first came to public attention in 1930, when his painting *American Gothic* won a medal at the Art Institute of Chicago. A year later he painted *The Midnight Ride of Paul Revere,* which makes no attempt at historical accuracy and, instead, has a dreamlike sense of unreality. The bird's-eye view makes the setting look like a New England town in miniature.

Listen my children and you shall hear / Of the midnight ride of Paul Revere, / On the eighteenth of April, in Seventy-five; / Hardly a man is now alive / Who remembers that famous day and year.

Groton School football team in Groton, Massachusetts, ca. 1920. Founded in 1884 by Reverend Endicott Peabody, Groton is one of the country's premiere preparatory schools.

A whale-ship was my Yale College and my Harvard.

The Friendship, built in Salem, Massachusetts in 1797. Oil painting by George Ropes, Jr., 1805.

Lobstermen, Maine, 1953. Ninety percent of the nation's lobster catch comes from Maine's coastal waters. Lobstermen harvest approximately forty million pounds of lobster a year. (Photo by Erich Hartmann)

Menu for New England Thanksgiving Dinner

Freedom From Want, by Norman Rockwell, 1943. Inspired by Franklin Delano Roosevelt's 1941 State of the Union address, Rockwell wanted to promote the concept of the four basic freedoms: of speech, of worship, from want, and from fear. Rockwell's third in the series, *Freedom from Want,* is one of his best-known illustrations. As beloved as the painting has become, however, Rockwell had concerns at the time that the image depicted overabundance, rather than want.

The people of the Penobscot Indian Nation are part of the Northeastern Woodlands tribes that are indigenous to Maine. Penobscot traditional dress included moccasins, cloaks with pointed hoods, breechcloths, and nose rings. In the early twentieth century, some of the natives would dress in ways that non-Indians identified as "Indian" (like George Ranco, pictured here in 1925) to attract tourists to buy their baskets and other crafts. To this day, the tribe inhabits the land where their forefathers lived before the arrival of the European settlers.

WELLESLEY

Members of the Wellesley College rowing crew on Lake Waban in Massachusetts, ca. 1950. (Photo by Orlando)

Lumbering in New England, ca. 1905. The lumber industry has a long history in Maine. Indigenous woods include varieties of pine, spruce, birch, and oak, along with hemlock and tamarack, among others. (Photo by Brown Brothers)

i thank You God for most this amazing day: for the leaping greenly spirits of trees and a blue true dream of sky; and for everything which is natural which is infinite which is yes.

Dominique Large Fowl Cock. Probably descended from the many hawk or gray fowls kept in New England before any poultry standards existed. The Dominique was admitted to the Standard of Perfection in 1874. (Photo by Tamara Staples)

Blueberry field in Autumn.
Washington County, Maine, 1995.
(Photo by Paul Rezendes)

*I*f we mean to have heroes, statesmen, and philosophers, we should have learned women.

Girls at Smith College in Northampton, Massachusetts, 1935. Heiress Sophia Smith left her fortune to establish the College, founded in 1871. A liberal arts college, Smith is among the largest privately endowed colleges for women in the United States. Noted alumnae include Sylvia Plath, Betty Friedan, Gloria Steinem, and Julia Child. (Photo by Toni Frissell)

The Landing of the Pilgrims at Plymouth, Massachusetts, Currier & Ives.

Young Maine fisherman.
(Photo by Rick Lew)

*W*hen a resolute young fellow steps up to the great bully, the world, and takes him boldly by the beard, he is often surprised to find it comes off in his hand, and that it was only tied on to scare away the timid adventurers.

Silver sugar urn, ca. 1790, by Paul Revere, Jr. (1735–1818), Boston, Massachusetts. American patriot Revere was an expert silversmith as well as an accomplished engraver, making him one of the few craftsmen who could complete an entire piece of silver, even to the engraved decoration.

Debutante ball at the Copley Plaza in Boston, Massachusetts, 1958. Debutantes in full-length white gowns and gloves are accepted into society. (Photo by Slim Aarons)

NEWPORT

Portrait of Luke B. Lockwood. Newport, Rhode Island, 1958. (Photo by Toni Frissell)

Red lobster. Long ago, lobsters were so plentiful that Native Americans used them to fertilize their fields and to bait their hooks for fishing. In colonial times, lobsters were considered "poverty food" and served to prisoners and indentured servants, some of whom rebelled putting into their contracts that they would not be forced to eat it more than three times a week.
(Photo by Davies + Starr)

Stylish New England clambake on a dock, 1952. The ritual predates New England. The Indians of Martha's Vineyard perfected this method of cooking food in a rock-lined sand pit long before the English, French, and Spanish crossed the Atlantic. (Photo by John Rawlings)

Jazz vocalist Velma Middleton performs with Louis Armstrong at the Newport Jazz Festival, ca. 1959. (Photo by Ted Williams)

Massachusetts-born John F. Kennedy, 1952. As president-elect, he said, "The enduring qualities of Massachusetts—the common threads woven by the Pilgrim and the Puritan, the fisherman and the farmer, the Yankee and the immigrant—will not be and could not be forgotten in the Nation's Executive Mansion. They are an indelible part of my life, my convictions, my view of the past, my hopes for the future."

*C*onventional wisdom not withstanding, there is no reason either in football or in poetry why the two should not meet in a man's life if he has the weight and cares about the words.

The Saturday Evening Post cover, November 1928. Illustrated by J. C. Leyendecker. Leyendecker's first cover for the magazine was in 1899, before the cover became a miniature poster designed to attract the eye of a newsstand buyer. In 1903 he returned to the publication for what was to be a forty-year association in which he produced over 320 covers.

Phillips Academy, Andover,
Massachusetts, 1969. Founded in
1778, Phillips Academy, better known
as Andover, is another one of New
England's prestigious preparatory
boarding schools. Although boys
wore coats and ties until 1969,
they are no longer required.
(Photo by Constantine Manos)

The house of my birth was quaint,
with clapboards running up and down,
neatly trimmed; there were five rooms,
a tiny porch, a rosy front yard,
and unbelievably delicious
strawberries in the rear.

Portrait of W. E. B. DuBois by Winold
Reiss, 1925. Massachusetts-born
and Harvard-educated, William
Edward Burghardt Du Bois was a
respected sociologist and historian
but he exerted his greatest influence
as a strategist in the early civil rights
movement. Along with Frederick
Douglass and Booker T. Washington,
he is considered one of the most
influential African Americans before
the civil rights movement.

Veteran marathoner Clarence DeMar
of the Melrose American Legion
Post crosses the finish line April 19,
1930 in Boston, Massachusetts, to
win the Boston Marathon for the last
of his record seven wins. DeMar's
time was 2:34:48.2.

The land is holy where they fought
And holy where they fell;
For by their blood that land was bought,
The land they loved so well.

Civil War Drum, Vermont Volunteers,
U.S. Infantry; ca.1860. The 9th
Regiment of Vermont Volunteers,
to whom this drum belonged, was
the first regiment organized under
the President's summons for help
to protect the national capital.